Thoughts

FROM A

Wolf

ERIC VANARSDALE

NEWMAN SPRINGS PUBLISHING
320 Broad Street
Red Bank, NJ 07701

First originally published by Newman Springs Publishing 2024

ISBN 979-8-88763-305-3 (Paperback)
ISBN 979-8-88763-306-0 (Digital)

Printed in the United States of America

To my family and friends who have helped me survive the many challenges of my life.

A special dedication to my children: Gabriel, Logan, and Julia. Thank you for being my constant positive.

Foreword

My dad is someone I look up to. He is a great father who has taught me many skills that I need in life. He has also taught me how important respect is, how to put others before myself, and how to overall be a good person. He is very easygoing and someone that I can always talk to and who has always been there for me. My dad is one of a kind.

—Gabriel

See, my dad isn't like the rest because he works hard and makes sure we are loved. Sometimes, we don't see him that much because he is working. He make jokes, and most of all, he tries his best to make sure that we have everything we need. He's a great dad, and I really hope you enjoy his writing."

—Logan

My dad is nice to my brothers and me. He likes to play games with me and watch me play with my toys. He tries as much as he can to spend time with us. He works at night, and he gets tired quickly, but he stays awake as much as he can to spend time with me.

—Julia

Time after Time

Time after time, she was there for me.
But many a time, when she would come to me,
All I could say was, "Oh gee!"
How could I be so cold, hard, tough, and cruel?
When she needed me through the years,
I ran away from her tears.
Why I do not know, but I wish I hadn't run away,
But toward her warm, soft, and tender heart.
'Cause now our time is cut short.
I'm sorry, my love, for not being there
When I saw that you needed me then.

Thank You

I don't know how to say it
But I owe a lot to you
I thank you for being there
When I felt that no one cared
I wish I could repay you for what you have done
But there isn't enough money or words to do so
So all that I can do
Is to say "Thank you!"
I wish I could say how I feel
When you are close by
Even when you don't say hi
The only way I can say thank you is by word on paper
I'm no longer good with words by mouth
It's really great to know that you care
Thank you for being there
For being there when I was scared, confused, and ready to give up
Thank you for being my friend!

Thoughts

My thoughts are like butterflies
They fly through the wind.
I have nothing to look forward to
Except for them to end.
There is always something to say,
and always something to do
I know I can't lie
So I will always be true.

Why

Why did I wait so long
To show my feelings to the one I love
Why did I wait till now
Why did I wait till she was leaving town
Why did I wait so long
To ask this beauty to come along
To live life happily,
Only if she wanted to be with me.
Why do I ask "Why?"
Because everything is done only in God's time

Beauty Bright

Your beauty burns so bright
All I can see is your light
When we are apart
I can feel my heart
Falling to pieces
When I am not in your arms, everything is dark
I can't see through the darkness
Unless you are around
Your beauty, I dare to compare
To what, there's nothing as fair
Why do I just stand and stare
At a beauty of such glory
That is yet another story.

Stinging Surprise

If you dare to linger
Then beware of a stinger.
Close your eyes,
I'll give you a surprise.
That when you reopen your eyes, you will realize,
What your surprise was.
Tell me your opinion.
Did you feel the sting,
Of my fervent embrace,
On your lips or your face.

Broken Vow

My mind is boggled
Oh, what should I do
I am dedicated to one
But I am in love with two
Oh, what should I do
Dedicated and true
I will always be with the one
Who is my sunshine,
Who gives me my smile
And is willing to go the extra mile,
Just to make me happy.
I wish she was near
To rid me of this fear.
This fear that is eating me away
In such a way that I cannot say
I wish I could clear my head
So I could go to bed
And sleep the whole night through
Or just be with you.

Caring Hand

Everyone comes to me
Whenever they are in need
But what about me
Who can I turn to when I am in need?
I met a friend
Who offered a caring hand
Not because I asked of it, nor for it
But because they saw I was in need
Just wanted to say "thanks!"
For offering your caring hand.

Confusion

Why does it always happen to me?
I fall in love, do something wrong, and then I lose the one I love.
Who can I turn to?
I'm so confused and don't know what to do.
I don't understand why!
Is it because I try too much?
Is it that I care too much?
Or maybe it is just me.
I wish I could go back in time to try it one more time,
But would it be the same, or would things change?
I don't know why, but I just want to cry,
Cry till my bad luck just passes me by.
Sometimes, I think the world would be great if I was never here.
Will things ever change?
I wish I could be what everyone wants me to be.
I'm so confused and don't know what to do.
Is the cause of this me or you?
I wish I knew what to do.
I'm so confused, oh what should I do?
I feel so alone, does anyone care?
I'm sitting in a group, but yet I still feel alone.
Who do I turn to, who do I talk to?
I just can't stand to see people hurt by things I do or say.
Would the world be better off without me?
I'm really confused!
Who do I turn to?
Where do I go?
Who do I trust?
I can't stand being confused anymore!

Drummer Boy

The rain's pitter-patter on the windowpane reminds me of a drummer boy.
O drummer boy so brave and small, marching forth to the battlefield followed by brave soldiers in blue.
First killed, last rewarded for his true bravery.
I will remember you always, brave drummer boy, when I hear the rain pitter-patter on the pane.
Alas, little drummer boy, you are rewarded…
Maybe not by a metal or a memorial,
But with bravery and honor.
Remember, brave drummer boy, you shall not be forgotten as long as the rain pitter-patters on my pane.
You might have been small in size, but big at heart.
So brave to lead the army to the fight,
Knowing that you might be the first to die.
You'll be remembered by me, little drummer boy.
Will I be remembered like you?
I do hope so, little drummer boy. Brave and true.

Explain

It wasn't nice
It wasn't right
I thought it was a dream
But it wasn't night
I don't want it like this
I want it to go away
I don't know what to say
I don't want it this way
I want to scream
I want to cry
I don't like this
I don't know why

Failure

I feel that I'm a failure—I can't seem to do anything right
I feel that I'm a failure—I always seem to cause a fight
I feel that I'm a failure—I always seem to hurt the ones I love the most
Am I a failure or do I just have bad luck?
Sometimes I feel like a failure—I always seem to start a fight
Can I do anything right?
Sometimes I feel like a failure—I always seem to hurt the ones I love
Is feeling like a failure good or bad?
Can I do anything right?
Maybe, but not tonight
Can I do anything right?

Fight or Write

I travel by day
And write by night
I write about the fight within
Will it ever end?
It seems as if it will carry on forever
Will I give up—never!
I will fight or write
Throughout the night
Continuing toward the light
Even though it seems to fade
I know that I am on my way
To a happier day

Forgive Me

Have I blown my chance
My chance at happiness
My love, give me another chance
To mend our fence
Please don't leave me now
Because I opened my mouth
Please forgive me
For what I said
Is our relationship dead
Did we just get a bump on the head
Did we hit a rough time
Did we bite into a lime
Oh, my sweet, please forgive me
For what I said
On the eve of our 90th day
Please forgive me for what I had to say
Please forgive me and allow us to stay
To stay together till the end of our days.

Going Away

Why does everything have to go away?
Just as you get used to something or someone, they go away.
Do I scare them away, or are they just wanting to get away from me?
Is it something I say or do, or is it just me in general?
Now that I found the one I truly love, is she going to go away too?
Why must everything go away?
The flowers in winter, the snow in spring, the rain after the sun comes out, the sun at night.
Is everything in my life going to leave me behind?
Why does everything have to go away?
Please don't leave me behind.

Heavenly Beauty

I met today
A heavenly beauty
That mended my heart of all shattered pieces
Oh, heavenly beauty
From where did you come
Is it from this earth or from beyond
When I saw your face
My life was changed
From bad to good
As if the seasons had changed
Heavenly beauty, I ask thee to stay
Only as long as your heart is filled with happiness
I will love thee forever
Oh, heavenly beauty.

He Is Here

Have you ever been scared
And did not know where to go
Just close your eyes
And think of the wind, the rain, and the snow
Think of the gentle breeze,
And the rain about to freeze.
God will be there waiting for you
Just say you love him, he will love you too.
You won't get too cold wherever you go
Just call upon God
And he will show up
Wherever you go.

A Lonely Tear

A lonely tear rolls down my cheek-
Seeping slowly into my mouth-
Heavily salted, rolling down my tongue-
A lonely tear rolls down my cheek-
All salty and sleek-
Trickles down onto my neck-
Down into a moist spot-
Around my collar-
Near my heart-
A lonely tear rolls down my cheek.

Lost Love

I lost my love because of friends
I found my love once again
I'm scared…Am I losing my love again?
Because of friends, maybe because I am not good enough anymore,
or maybe I'm too good.
If I lose my love again, will I ever find it again?
It's hard to tell whether I'm going to fail in keeping my found-lost
love or not.
I hope I'm not too late—have I lost my love?

Night

All through the night
I feel that I'm involved in a fight
Not with my parents
Not with my girlfriend
But who and why?
All through the night
My muscles are tight
From my head to my toes
As the pain comes and goes
From the fight
In which I don't know my foes
All through the night
I ask myself, who could they be?
Is it God?
Is it Satan?
Is it my mind?
Or is it my body?
All though the night
I feel that I'm in a fight
My muscles are tight
Oh, who or what could it be
That is fighting me?

Our Love

Day in and day out
How I long to shout it out
To shout how true my love is for you
To tell the world how you make me feel
Though I am not worthy of your beauty
Nor do I deserve your love
Our love came by, only by chance
We choose to climb and explore on this branch
Thus opened the door
To take a glance
At the most beautiful person in my midst
Our love is strange and has lasted through a range
A range of experiences in feelings, thoughts, and pleasures
And though a range of troubles and trials
Alas, through this we have survived
Thus strengthening us in many ways.
Every time I hear your voice or even your name,
I can't help but smile
To smile the smile that you gave to me.

Out

I hold it in
Although I want to let it out
I just want to shout
I know if I don't let it out
That I might explode
Alas, I feel that if I do let it out
That *no one* will care
What should I do
I can't win nor lose
I can't stand it
I think I am going to lose it
Even though I don't choose it
I don't know what will happen
Either way
I need a way
To let it go
Whether it is by a shout or a tear
I need to get it out
Before it rips me apart
Or before I shatter someone's heart who is very near to me.

I'm Sorry

I'm sorry—I use it a lot
I'm sorry—I can't seem to keep you happy anymore
I'm sorry—If I caused you any trouble
I'm sorry—I keep causing you to be angry
I'm sorry—I can't make it right
Sometimes, all that comes to my mind when a situation goes wrong
is "I'm sorry"
I'm sorry—I use this phrase a lot
I'm sorry for a lot

Special One

All night long
All I can do is long for you.
The way you tell me what's on your mind.
Sends shivers up my spine.
You're always on my mind.
I hear a song that reminds me of you.
I can't help but to wish to be able to hold you,
In my arms, the whole night through.
When you talk, I'm comforted.
When you sing, I'm calmed.
When I see you, my heart persists on beating my chest.
When you're in my arms all snuggled and warm, I can't help but guess,
If you're gonna be mine forever.
Then you look at me with your beautiful eyes,
And I know that we were meant to be together, maybe forever.
When I kiss your lips, so soft and sweet, I feel that I'm not standing on my feet,
But on a thin layer of air.
I feel sometimes as if we are one. I will love you forever, my special one.

A Father's Sacrifice

A choice had to be made.
Of which I am worried about the consequence.
To provide for you needs, or spend time with you as you grow.
I hope you'll understand
The choice that I choose.
I gave up time with you.
So you could be taken care of.
I had to take a second job,
This is not going to be fun.
Unfortunately, it had to be done,
At least I know your necessities will be met,
The older and bigger you get.
Our time together will be cut short for now,
But only for a little while.
Soon I will be able to spend more time with you,
Once our finances are renewed.
I wanted you to know,
Your smile helps keep me going.
Even though I struggle to fight back my tears,
I still will whisper "I love you" to you,
When I get to hold you in my arms or while I am watching you sleep.
Knowing that somehow you understand,
What I have to do is the right thing to do.
I hope that my decision will provide a good example,
For you when you become a man and have a family of your own.

Fatherhood

I woke one morning and felt something new.
It was a feeling that I would be seeing you soon.
I have dreamed about you for a while,
Every time, I would wake with a smile.
Soon you will be here, and I can hold you near.
Almost nine months have passed,
And you are on your way.
Your life is about to start,
But already you have touched my heart.
Your birth didn't happen as planned,
You didn't want to come out.
The doctors started gently pulling,
And you were about to appear.
One your head was out,
I just wanted to shout.
You started to cry,
And honestly, so did I.
Two of my greatest dreams were coming true.
The first was with your mom,
And now the second with the three of you.
Every day is a new adventure,
Every moment makes a memory.
You have already grown so much,
Since the day you joined us.
Daily you are getting stronger,
You will be crawling or even walking before much longer.
Even on my worst days,
Your cute laugh makes me smile.
No matter what,

I will always try to go the extra mile.
To provide for you,
Or just be there for you.
You can talk to me about anything, anytime.
I am glad I am your father and that you are my children.

Addiction

It started shortly after the first time
Now I can't get it out of my mind.
I want it so bad,
When I can't get it, I just get mad.
I have tried a little of this and a little of that.
Some of which I enjoy alone,
Others I share.
Some I dream of, but would never dare.
I am scared.
What will people think?
What will they say?
I've expressed my addiction with only a few,
Oh, if certain people only knew.
My addiction haunts me,
Or maybe it is just a flicker of my imagination.
When my eyes gaze upon nature's design,
I want to join in and free my mind.
The musty smell of nature's oasis,
The mental image of prior, future, or even fantasy fixes
Causes an increase of what I want.
The sensations and urges only seem to get stronger,
The longer time passes from its start.
My addiction is weighing hard on my heart.
I wish it would go away,
But I demand it to stay.
I'm trying to master it,
But occasionally I'm willing to let it thrive.
Oh, this strange addiction of mine.

Breaking Point

I have tried so hard for so long to keep my head held high.
As my burden is growing, today I broke.
Uncontrollable waves of tears streaming down my face.
I hurt so bad,
The loneliness is slowly killing me.
My kids are my positive.
I continue to push forward without a guide.
I am growing weaker.
Soon I won't be able to hide.
Where should I go?
Is anyone there?
I rarely get to release, sometimes not for weeks.
The fog is so thick now.
The concept of failure is biting hard at my mind,
Reinforced by the players in this game…
I strive to be my best, but seem to constantly fall short.
The mental poison has corrupted my mind,
I broke today.
It's getting hard to concentrate, sleep is so sparce.
I have to keep up the good face…
I fight so the world will never know.

Noniversary

These two days will always have a place in my heart,
Even if now they only cause pain.
Things will never be the same.
The third we started our love, the fourth our marriage began.
I am struggling with these couple of dates,
As our love has been destroyed by our fate.
We are still in the same house,
But could not be further apart.
My head hangs low
And I fight back the occasional burst of tears.
Twenty-three years of our lives we have shared together.
Times were once better,
Now it seems to pass, rather fast.
My daily life is a torrent of emotion,
Some good, most painful.
I put on a mask to hide it all away.
What is left to say?
To struggle through another day.

Alone

Times are tough,
And I only trust a few.
To talk about my daily view.
The bantering got harsh,
So I pushed away and retreated…
Now I feel alone.
I hate being alone,
But this time, it was necessary.
I have decided that I am going to push forward in the current process.
I'll make the necessary changes,
And attempt again to obtain the required cooperation from you.
I will foot the bill,
Just to proceed up the hill.
We will have to live as roommates,
Until other arrangements can be made.
I have given up,
I can't do this anymore.
I want to be allowed to be happy.
I feel like I am dying more every day. You are allowed to go hang out
or do things with whoever,
But I am strongly imprisoned by my vows.
I have no one to talk to,
No one to bounce thoughts or feelings off of.
I feel alone.
I am just lonely, so I am quilling my thoughts to relieve the pressure.
Where do I go from here?
I feel so alone!

The Crow and the Rose

The crow flies low through a field,
Its shadow grows larger as it passes a rose,
A petal falls softly to the ground,
The petal bends a blade of grass till it gives way.
The color slowly fades,
As the days go by,
Back to dust, it slowly turns
Not even a gentle rain can ease its pain.
The crow swoops up to the clouds
Raindrops graze its back,
All shiny and black,
Falling gracefully to the ground
To bring the dust to life.
A river forms and flows through the valley,
A torrent of trees and debris,
The crow glides down low,
To watch the shiny show.
A glint of light,
Caresses the waves,
Teasing the crow for days.
The crow flies low,
And smiles at the rose.

Galaxy

Looking into your eyes
A glimmer of light
Not a reflection
But a tiny galaxy.
With light and darkness in a balanced embrace.
Spinning all through the age,
Representative of all things good and bad
That have been experienced,
A spiral of mystery,
A guiding light.
Floating on the tears
From all the years,
Happy and sad.
Good and bad.
The balance must be kept by a celestial being.
Bringing our life meaning.
Look into my eyes
For a unique view,
Of the galaxy that guides my heart
Since my earthly start.

Newest Adventure

Decided to embark on a new adventure,
To let my voice be heard.
I write down my thoughts,
No matter how absurd.
I share a glimmer of my soul.
My words have helped me,
Get through the darkest of times,
And remind me of the best.
What comes next,
I don't know.
I want this adventure,
The time has come to shine,
On this world of mine.
Positive and negative,
Are both required
To have a balance of needs and desires.
The tasks will not be easy,
But worth the wait.

The Rose of Friendship

I give you this rose of friendship as a token of my appreciation for offering your friendship and assistance on the variety of levels that you have been able to offer during my present and future times of need. With this rose of friendship, I also offer my friendship and assistance to you should you ever need it.

The stem—Strength that grows stronger as the journey of friendship travels through the years

The thorns—Offers protection from those forces out to destroy us all

The branch of leaves—Offers help and assistance like an outstretched hand

The blossom—The fruit of the labor involved in making and keeping great friends

The petals—Developed to be soft and gentle from the kindness of a true friend

Blame Game

Through the years
And many tears
I have been
Constantly forced to take the blame
This is no game
Everything I have tried
Only seems to make it worse
I finally saw the light
After a huge fight
I now see it as a form or abuse
That you always seem to use
I have had my fill
And refuse to take it anymore
I'm closing the door
We are now separated
I am kinda elated
Still stuff to finalize
I hope you will realize
I am not willing to participate
In this game of constant blame
From this day forward

Trust

It is hard for me to give it to anyone,
I have been betrayed by so many.
I cherish it like precious gems, gold, or silver
I am willing to fight to protect it,
Between those whom I call friends.
For me, it is so fragile,
Easily ripped to shreds.
If I suspect that it has been breached,
One chance you will get to save it,
Though it will never be the same.
Trust is a big thing for me,
I advise you to not mess with it.
Once it is gone, it will never be won again.
I give it to only a few,
Because it has been lost by so many.

Twinkle from Afar

The sun has set for the night
The temperature is just right
I go for a stroll
It's beautiful outside.
The moon is not out,
So the stars shine bright,
In the vastness of the night.
Tonight only one catches my eye
More than the others
It seems to dance,
I continue to glance toward it,
And watch it twinkle.

Positive Flame

I once displayed a constant flame
That always presented the positive.
My positive flame grew dim
Due to life circumstances.
It was nearly extinguished
And the darkness began to take control
Negativity and low self-esteem were daily projections.
Recently, an epiphany
And the flame began to grow and gather strength again.
The warmth radiates furthermore.
I strive to share its warmth as often as I can throughout the day.
In its glow, I can start to see changes.
I am not letting go this time,
I will let it burn bright,
So others will experience its warmth and light.
My new flame may flicker,
But will continue to grow strong.
A positive influence I want to become
Strong and bright to God's gracious delight.

Love—the Verb

So many get caught up in the saying,
But it takes more to meet the requirements for *love*.
The level of sincerity is enforced…
With just some action, of course, for it to count.
Let us not discount that love is defined as a verb,
Not just a saying or a feeling.
Action is required to share this emotion,
To put a heart in motion.
A simple touch, a hug, or even a kiss,
Shows what you mean,
More than words could do alone.
Love requires action,
For you to get satisfaction.

The Array

In front of the array,
I sit past the end of the day.
The lines trace by,
Left to right.
I can watch up to seventy-two,
With this, the stress is extremely high.
I constantly hope,
That none of them die.
Some are fast,
Others are slow, some just say it's time to go,
While others put on a grand show.
I watch an array of five,
Some days, I cannot lie,
I wish it were less.
I watch with care,
As they all rest.

My Boys

When they were born,
I knew they were both going to be unique.
Both are growing to be strong young men,
Eager to help whenever they can.
My boys make me proud,
As I watch them grow to be men.
I strive to be there for them,
As often as I can.
To each, I feel a special bond,
Through the life events that we have worked through.
This road that we are on,
Has at times been very bumpy,
While other times, it has been rather smooth.
We stride together,
As each day is renewed.

A Lantern

A lantern is lit
With its wick ever long,
Illuminates the night
Ever so bright.
Carried, hung, or floating in the air,
Floods light everywhere.
It guides us on our journey,
Through a darkened path.
By morning light,
We made it through the night.
Time to start our day,
With the light, now here to stay.

A Little Note

I carry a little note,
Given to me by my daughter.
It talks about how being sad and alone at times is a possibility,
But for me not to get too sad,
Because she loves me no matter how far apart we are.
She says, "Just take out this note, and smile for a while,
Because I will see you in a little while."
I carry a little note,
That makes me smile, until I get to hug my child.

Honesty

I have always said,
It means a lot to me.
And I have told my children,
To cherish it too.
I held something from them,
And was not totally true.
Honesty is the answer, and now I want to make it right.
There has been a lot of discussion,
And a decision has been made.
Regardless of what you have been told,
Time has taken its toll,
Divorce is in the future.
Everything is just a mess,
I wish I was strong enough to tell you sooner,
But I want to be honest,
I have held this double burden for long enough.
Not being honest,
And the decision for a change to our family.
Honesty is the key.
I'm gonna be honest with you,
So you can be honest with me.

Rebirth

I've been emotionally scourged and beaten for oh so long,
A seed was planted by a foreigner that came along,
I will live this way no longer a day.
I grow stronger with every day,
To fight the evil that I now live with today.
Soon I'll be strong enough to walk away.
A love forever, once was promised.
A change has yet taken it away.
Soon my happiness will be reborn.

About the Author

Eric VanArsdale was born on January 12, 1981, in Wichita, Kansas. He started writing poetry in high school and continues to write today. He uses poetry to help cope with different stressful and emotional situations throughout his life and hopes that his poetry might provide guidance or inspiration to others. Eric enjoys spending time with his three children, drawing, and watching movies. Eric is currently working in the field of medicine as a Cardiac Monitor Technician, and he has a previous employment background in law enforcement as well.